Kathleen Wood

The Cry of a Dog

Illustrated by Colin Wheeler

Hart-Davis Educational

Granada Publishing Limited
Hart-Davis Educational Limited
First published in 1974 by Hart-Davis Educational Limited
Frogmore, St. Albans, Hertfordshire
Reprinted 1976

ISBN 0 247 12522 9

Printed by
Acorn Typesetting & Litho Services Ltd.
634 River Gardens, Feltham, Middx.

1

It all began
with the cry of a dog.

Alan heard it
one Sunday afternoon
as he sat by the river.
It came from behind him.
From out of the dark wood.
From under the green still trees.

It was a cry for help.
The cry of a dog in pain.

Alan was seventeen.
He had found this quiet spot
six weeks ago.
And now each Sunday afternoon
he cycled here.

He did not come to fish.
He just came to lie around.
He wanted to be on his own.
He had had quite enough
by Sunday afternoon.

His father kept a shop
on a housing estate.
He sold almost everything
from butter and bread
to cigarettes and papers.

Alan had always lived
in the four small rooms above it.
It was not like a home at all.
Most of the time
his mother was in the shop.

She was always busy,
even when the shop was shut.
Busy cooking hams
and baking cakes to sell.

Alan's father
was always working too.
And when he talked to Alan
it was about the shop.

For years now
Alan had helped with the papers.

When he was still at school
he got up at six o'clock.
He had the paper round to do.
And at night
there was always something else.

"There you are at last, Alan!"
his father would say.
"Give me a hand with these boxes!"

Or his mother would call out:
"Is that you, Alan?
Where *have* you been?
You know Mrs White
wants her goods by five o'clock!"

Now that he had left school
it went on all day.
Alan, do this. . . . Alan, do that. . . .
He was sick of it.

But here
on the cold green grass
under the blue and open sky
he could forget about it.

Here he could watch
the sun on the water.
Here he could listen
for the larks above the field.

2

He had never wanted
to work in a shop.
He had wanted to be a footballer.

When he was only nine
he played for the school.
Every evening
he went out with a ball.
And in the street
he learnt to head it.

He was tall for his years.
They used to laugh at him
and call him Lanky.
But they soon found
he could head the ball.
And they never laughed again.

When he left school
he played for a Youth Club.
He played for them
on Sunday mornings.

Some men
from the Town Football Club
sometimes stood around.

Once he heard them talking:
"That boy wants watching.
We could do with a lad like him."

Then one week
they had a word with him:
"We would like to try you out.
Come along
on Saturday afternoon."

Alan raced home.
His chance had come at last.
He would show them!
He always knew he was good.

Some outside steps
led to the rooms above the shop.
He took them two at a time.

He opened the door.
"Dad!" he cried.
"They are going to try me out
on Saturday afternoon!"

His father was reading the paper.
He looked up.
His mother was cooking the dinner.
She turned round at once.

"Saturday afternoon?" she cried.
"You must be out of your mind!
How can you play
on Saturday afternoon?"

Alan looked at her.
"It's not fair," he said.
"I want to play on Saturdays.
It's your shop.
You could pay some one
to help in it."

"Don't you talk to me like that!"
his mother cried.
"I work my fingers
to the bone for you.
And that's all the thanks I get!"

His father put the paper down.
''Come on, Alan,'' he said.
''Don't take on like that.
You know your mother by now.
You had better do what she says.''

Yes. Alan *did* know his mother.
He still played on Sundays.
But the game
didn't seem to matter any more.
And soon he gave it up.

''I have had my chance,''
he was thinking
that afternoon by the river.
''I have had my chance
and lost it.''
But he did not know
what was to come.

3

It all began
with this cry of a dog.
Alan was almost asleep.
He opened his eyes and listened.

It came again.
This cry for help.
This cry of a dog in pain.

He jumped up and ran.
He came to the trees.
He heard dry sticks
break under his feet.

The wood was quiet as a church.
The air was green and cold.
Plants grew across his path
as he followed the cry.
He had to pull at them
to get at the dog.

It was a black and white spaniel.
He could not get away
because of the trap.

When he saw Alan
he began to paw the ground.
But it hurt too much
And he soon had to stop.

Alan went down on his knees.
It did not take long
to open the trap.

The dog pressed his wet nose
into his hands.
One of his back paws
was hanging down.
It was wet with blood.
There was blood too
on his long soft ears.

Alan read the name
round his neck:
PADDY HILL FARM
near HAYFORD

He picked the dog up.
"Come on, Paddy!" he cried.
Then he made his way back
to the river.

He knew where Hill Farm was.
He passed it every Sunday.
It was about half a mile away.
He left his cycle in the wood.
Then he set off down the road.

The dog grew heavy in his arms.
Once he stopped to rest them.
"Come on, Paddy!" he said.
"See if you can walk now!"
But the dog just sat
and looked at him.

At last they reached the farm.
As Alan went through the gates
he heard steps behind him.
Some one called out, "Here!
What's the matter with Paddy?"

Alan turned round.
He saw a boy of about his own age.
It was Keith Roberts
from the farm.

"Paddy's heavy," Keith said.
"Let me have him.
Where did you find him?"
Alan told him all about it.
"He *will* go to the woods," Keith said.
"We have found him there before."

At last they reached the house.
They cleaned Paddy's paw.
Then they gave him
something to eat.

By the time
they had finished
Alan felt
he had known Keith all his life.

4

Keith's mother and father
came in from the yard.
They said Alan must stay to tea.
Keith's Uncle Tom
was there as well.
They all sat down together.
The shop seemed far away.

After tea
the two boys went outside.

There was a football
lying in the yard.
Alan began playing with it.
So they took it to the fields.

Keith saw at once
how good Alan was.
He saw he could do
what he liked with a ball.

As for Alan,
it was great to feel the ball again.
To feel it at his feet.

He took it down the field.
He could see Keith coming for it.
So he side-stepped
and passed him in a second.
He raced on down the field.
The ball seemed part of him.

Keith's father and his Uncle Tom
came into the field.
They stood by the gate
and watched.
But Alan didn't see them.
His eyes were on the ball.

He slowed down.
He passed the ball to Keith.
Keith sent it high into the air.

Alan jumped for it
and headed it back.
Then he saw
some one else in the field.
It was Uncle Tom.

After that
it was between Alan
and Keith's uncle.
They took the ball
down the field together.

Keith came out.
But it was no good.
They passed him every time.

At last
they went over to the gate.
"Well, Tom," Keith's father said.
"What do you make of him?"

Uncle Tom laughed.
"Make of him?" he cried.
"He's just the lad I'm looking for."

It turned out that Uncle Tom
ran the Hayford Football Club.
"We need some one like you,"
he said to Alan.
"Come along next Saturday.
You shall have a game with us."

"I'll come with you,"
Keith told Alan.
"But I don't play myself.
Uncle Tom
gave me up long ago!"

5

It was getting late
when Alan left the farm.
Keith went with him
as far as the wood.

The trees stood dark and still.
The singing larks had gone.
The sun was red over the river.

Alan thought
of Paddy's cry for help.
It seemed so long ago.

He found his cycle
under the trees.
"See you on Saturday,"
he called back
as he set off for home.
He still had to face his mother.
But it didn't seem to matter now.

He had found a friend.
His mother must do without him.

She must find some one else
to help in the shop.
Some one for Saturday afternoons.

His second chance had come.
He must not miss it.